EXPLORE!

by Janine Wheeler
Illustrated with photographs

HAMPTON-BROWN

Weather in Many Places

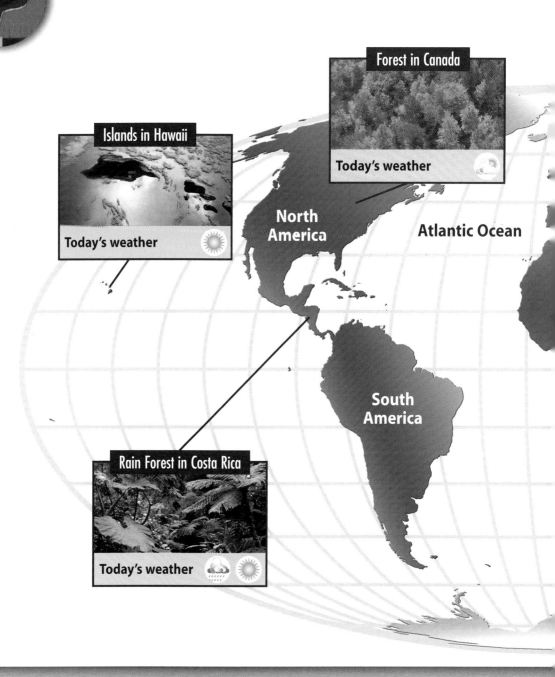

Forest in Canada

Today's weather

Islands in Hawaii

Today's weather

North America

Atlantic Ocean

South America

Rain Forest in Costa Rica

Today's weather

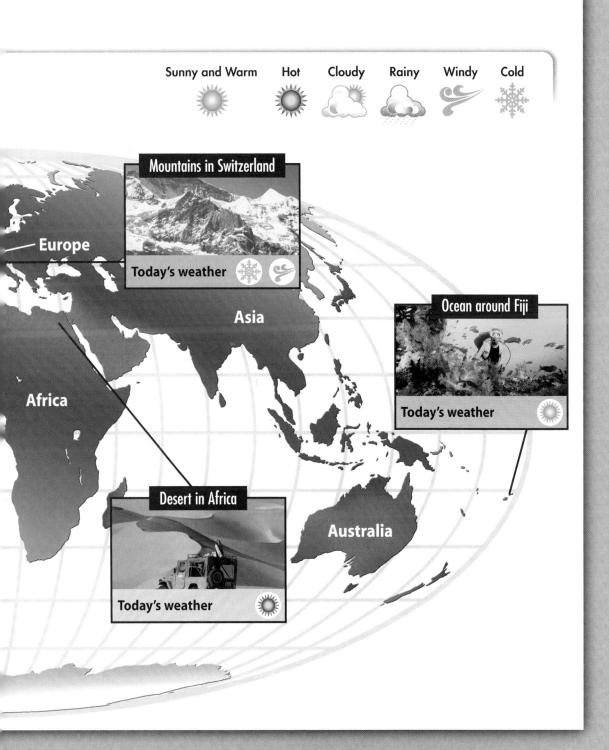

Sunny and Warm · Hot · Cloudy · Rainy · Windy · Cold

Mountains in Switzerland

Europe

Today's weather

Asia

Ocean around Fiji

Today's weather

Africa

Desert in Africa

Today's weather

Australia

EXPLORE!

TAKE A BIKE!
EXPLORE THE FOREST!

You can look at
the beautiful leaves.

You can listen
to wolves!

You can search
for birds.

Dress for cool weather!

helmet

vest

shirt

Take a plane!
Explore an island!

You can count the
colors of the rainbow.

You can fly with
the birds.

You can watch a volcano.

Dress for warm weather!

cap

shorts

sandals

TAKE A RAFT!
EXPLORE THE RAIN FOREST!

You can find a frog.

You can smell the flowers.

You can meet some monkeys.

  **Dress for rain!**

 jacket

long pants

  shoes

Take a jeep!
Explore the desert!

You can look
for sheep.

You can stop to
touch the sand.

Dress for hot weather!

hat

shorts

socks

You can spot
a camel.

11

TAKE A BOAT!
EXPLORE THE OCEAN!

You can
meet a starfish.

You can swim
with the fish.

You can search
for a crab.

You can discover
the coral reef.

Dress for swimming!

diving
mask

swim trunks

TAKE A TRAIN!
EXPLORE THE MOUNTAINS!

You can take a picture.

You can hike through the mountains.

You can greet a cow.

Dress for snow!

scarf

parka

boots

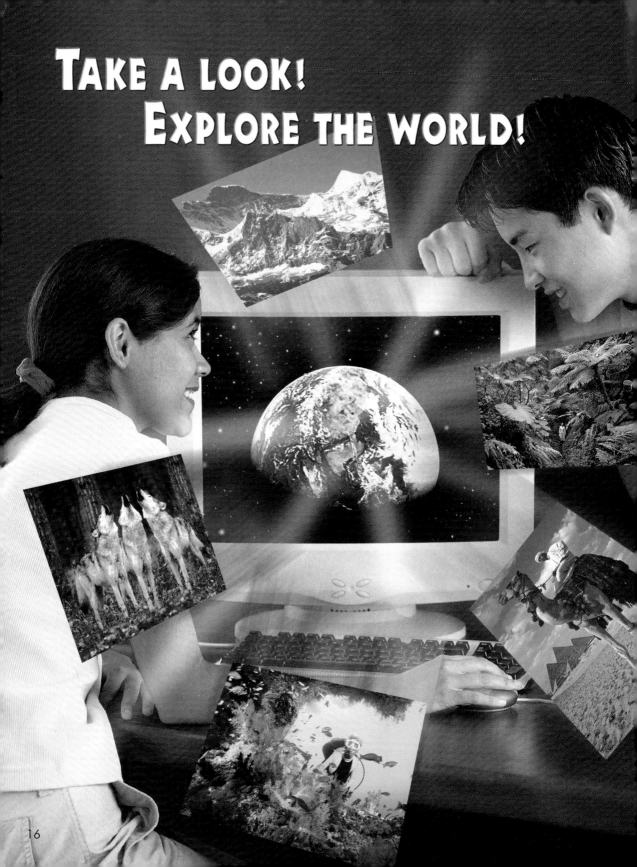

TAKE A LOOK!
EXPLORE THE WORLD!